Property of
O'Hara Gurstein
San Jose, Calif.

PRACTICAL

URINALYSIS

FOR NURSES

BY

E. W. MARQUARDT, M. D.
Attending Obstetrician to the German Hospital
of Chicago.

CHICAGO MEDICAL BOOK CO.

CHICAGO
1912

PREFACE.

The fact that urinalysis is of so much importance, made it seem advisable to place before the nurses and students, a short and comprehensive treatise on this subject, so often neglected especially by the nurses. Therefore an effort was made to crystallize the thought brought forth in a series of lectures on the subject, that it may be of service for ready reference. Since it is intended as an elementary treatise, various theories have not been fully discussed, nor have the chemical problems been thoroughly fathomed. However, the various points have been elucidated according to the simplest modern theories.

In the preparation of this, including the sketches I have to thank my colleague Dr. C. v. Bachelle.

E. W. MARQUARDT, M. D.,

Ex-Interne German Hospital of Chicago.

Chicago, Ill., June 16, 1902.

PREFACE TO SECOND EDITION.

The demand for this book far exceeding the expectation of the authors, has led to a call for a second edition in which we have added materially to the text and illustrations, incorporating some of the more modern ideas and methods of technique.

Hoping that it will continue to be a satisfactory text book for nurses and beginners, and should this volume be the means of lightening their work, the authors will feel well rewarded for their efforts.

I am under many obligations to Dr. C. v. Bachelle for his valuable suggestions in the preparation of this volume.

E. W. MARQUARDT, M. D.

Chicago, Nov., 1910.

URINALYSIS.

The examination of the urine is of great service in diagnosis of disease.

In order that it shall be complete, it is necessary to have a specimen of a twenty-four hour mixture, to be examined physically, chemically and microscopically.

In order to be in a position to discuss these questions intelligently, it is well first of all to consider the manner in which urine is formed and eliminated and the organs connected with this process.

The kidneys are two bean shaped organs situated deeply in the lumbar region on either side of the spinal column. They correspond in position to the last two dorsal and two upper lumbar vertebrae, the right being slightly lower than the left, on account of the liver. They are about four inches long, two and one-half inches broad and one and a half inches thick and the weight is about four and one-half ounces.

The kidney is surrounded by an outer tough fibrous capsule which can easily be stripped off. When the kidney is cut it presents a central cavity known as the pelvis, which is formed by the upper dilated part of the ureter. This cavity divides into several tubular divisions called infundibula. This is surrounded on all sides by the kidney substance except at the notch or hilum. The kidney consists of two parts, an external or cortical and an internal called the medullary porton. The cortical portion is situated beneath the capsule and has a bright reddish-brown color, and is soft

and granular to the touch. The medullary portion is
of a pale, reddish color and consists of striated conical
masses, called from their shape, the pyramids.

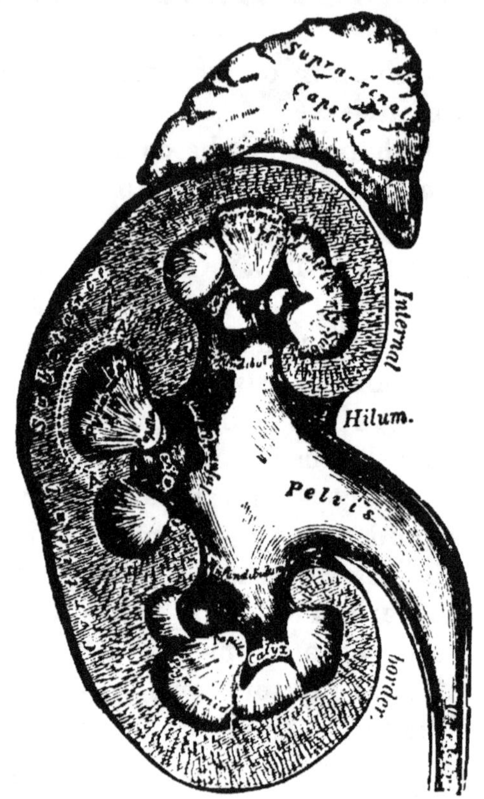

Vertical Section of Kidney, from Gray's Anatomy

The kidney is made up mainly of malpighian bodies, small tubes, fatty tissue and blood vessels. The
malpighian bodies are small rounded masses, of a deep
red color and about 1-120 inch in diameter and found
only in the cortical portion. They consist of a net-
work of blood vessels called the glomerulus, which is
surrounded by a fine membrane known as Bowman's
or malpighian capsule. The tubules are small channels

commencing in the malpighian bodies. In the cortical portion they are very tortuous, but in the pyramids they are quite straight in their direction, and open by small orifices which discharge their contents into the central cavity or pelvis. These tubules consist of an outer membrane which is lined by epithelial cells.

The kidney receives its blood supply from the renal artery which is a branch of the aorta, and the blood is returned by the renal vein which opens into the inferior vena cava.

The ureters are two tubes which conduct the urine from the kidneys to the bladder. They lead from the pelvis of the kidney and pass downward and inward to the posterior and inferior part of the bladder, where they open by constricted orifices. The ureter is a cylindrical membranous tube about sixteen inches in length and of the diameter of a goose quill. It has three coats, an outer fibrous, the middle, muscular and an inner which consists of mucous membrane.

The bladder is the reservoir for the urine. It is situated in the pelvis, behind the pubic bone, in front of the rectum in the male, and in front of the uterus in the female. When it is empty it is Y shaped, when moderately full it has a rounded form and when fully distented it is oval in shape and rises into the abdominal cavity. It consists of four coats, an outer serous, underneath a muscular, then submucous and an inner mucous. When moderately distended it holds about a pint.

The urethra is a narrow canal about an inch and a half in length in the female and eight to nine in the male, extending from the neck of the bladder, passing underneath the pubic bone to the meatus urinarius.

It consists of three coats, an outer muscular, a middle spongy and the inner of mucous membrane.

The function of the kidney is to separate from the blood certain materials which when dissolved in a quantity of water, also taken from the blood by the kidneys, constitutes the urine. Therefore the urine is an excretion from the kidneys.

The urine is formed by two process, viz.: 1. Filtration 2. Secretion.

Filtration is performed within the malpighian body by the glomerulus, by which the water and ready-formed salts are strained off and the quantity filtered off depends largely upon the blood pressure in these glomeruli, i. e. the greater the blood pressure the greater will be the quantity of urine separated and vice versa, but this will be again referred to.

Secretion is partly performed by the epithelial cells which line the tubules, and which separate from the blood such substances as urea, and is not dependent upon blood pressure, but upon the activity of these cells. Urea is also formed in the liver from the amido-acids which reach it after they are absorbed from the digestive tract and also by the rearrangement of the molecules of certain ammonium salts. It is believed that nearly all the parenchymatous organs and the muscles share in the formation of urea, so that there is no one organ that has alone such an important function as that of manufacturing urea.

After the urine has been formed in the kidney it passes slowly into the ureter and enters the bladder drop by drop.

EXAMINATION OF URINE.

In order to obtain the most accurate results it is best to examine a specimen from a 24 hours mixture, because it varies in composition from hour to hour.

The morning urine is generally strongly acid in reaction and highly colored i. e. dark, while the evening urine is usually the opposite. If a 24 hours specimen cannot be obtained, then that of the middle of the day is best for examination.

The way to collect a 24 hours specimen is as follows:

Upon arising in the morning empty the bladder and note the exact time. Collect all the urine for 24 hours i. e. to the same time the next morning and empty the bladder again. The bladder must be empty at the beginning of the count and emptied at the end of the 24 hours.

The vessel in which the urine is to be collected must be well cleansed or better, sterilized and kept covered in a cool place, so that no dust or other foreign particles may enter the urine. About 4 fl. oz. should be sent to the laboratory and we may then begin to study it.

Normal urine is a perfectly clear and transparent liquid, with a peculiar odor and of mildly acid reaction. On standing for a short time a little mucous appears as a flocculent cloud which entangles any minute particles, as dust. This may be looked upon as perfectly normal, but any other sediment or deposit must be considered as abnormal.

The Color—The color normally varies from a light

straw to a reddish yellow. What this coloring is due to is not exactly known, but we may call it urochrome.

The chief factors in the variability of color are 1. Peculiarities of persons. 2. Diet. 3. Quantity.

The color varies inversely as the quantity. Some individuals normally pass a lighter or darker urine than others. It is more likely to be increased by a meat diet than by a vegetable diet.

Drugs like Rhubarb and Senna impart a brown or darker color.

Saccharine and chloride of gold give it a brilliant orange color.

Carbolic acid will give it a smoky appearance. Methylene blue when given internally will give it a blue color.

The Color in Diseases.

Increased: Fever. Liver trouble. Melanotic tumors.

Decreased: Diabetes (saccharine and insipid). Hysteria and other nervous affections. Fibroid kidney.

The Odor—Normal urine has a characteristic odor, which is due to various ethers in it. It varies in intensity and inversely as the quantity. It is also influenced by diet, as the taking of onions, turpentine or cubebs will impart characteristic odors. In fever patients it has a somewhat peculiar odor, known as "fever urine odor." In saccharine diabetes it is rather pleasant and resembles new mown hay. When it resembles ammonia it indicates that ammoniacal decomposition has taken place.

The Quantity—The quantity of urine passed in 24 hours varies, but as a rule it is about 40 fl. oz. or 1250 c.c. However, it is subject to considerable variation. Women and children as a rule pass less than men, and as old age advances the amount decreases to about 35 fl. oz. Whenever there is an increased ingestion of large amounts of liquids as water, beer or milk, it will cause an increase in the quantity. However, if the food is dry, and small amounts of liquids are taken, the flow of the urine will be diminished. Loss of water from other parts of the body is an important factor, therefore, the quantity depends largely upon the activity of the skin and the bowels.

In profuse perspirations and in diarrhea the quantity will be diminished, because there is loss of water from other parts of the body than the kidneys. If there is chilling of the skin whereby free perspiration is diminished the quantity of urine increases therefore, larger amounts are passed in winter than in summer.

Anything that causes a rise in blood pressure will increase the flow of urine and this may be brought about by, 1. Increase of heart's action; 2. Constriction of small vessels; 3. Division of renal nerve; it is diminished by, 1. Weak heart's action; 2. Dilatation of small vessels; 3. Constriction of renal artery.

Quantity in Diseases.

Increased:	Diminished:
Cardiac hypertrophy, Dibetes (saccharine and insipid), Hysteria and many other nervous affections, interstitial nephritis, Absorption of œdema.	Febrile disturbances, Acute nephritis, Chronic nephritis, Shock after operation.

Specific Gravity—The specific gravity of urine is taken for the purpose of ascertaining the amount of solids contained in solution and this is most easily determined by an instrument called urinometer. The specific gravity varies in normal urine between 1015-1025.

If a specimen is presented for an examination slightly warm or cool it until it assumes the temperature of the room, as this gives the most accurate results, since the instrument is adjusted to this temperature. If the urine is cold, the specific gravity will be accordlingly increased, and visa versa.

To take the specific gravity, place a sufficient quantity of urine in a small vessel large enough to allow the urinometer to float without touching the sides of the vessel, let it come to a standstill, and read off the specific gravity from the bottom of the meniscus.

In order to calculate the total solids the specific gravity must be taken off a 24 hour mixture, because it varies from hour to hour. Therefore the calculation based upon one micturition would be valueless.

The total solids in the urine may be determined by Haines' co-efficient (1.1) as follows:

Take the specific gravity and multiply the last two figures of the specific gravity by 1.1, this gives the number of grains in one fl. oz.; then multiply this by the number of fl. oz. passed, which will give the number of grains in 24 hours.

Example 1020=specific gravity, 40 fl. oz. passed. 20x1.1=22.0 grains in one fl. oz. 22x40=880 grains in 24 hours.

The total solids in an adult of an average size, weight diet and exercise is about 950 grains in 24 hours. The total solids vary considerably with the diet. A meat diet will increase, and a vegetable diet will diminish them. A small person eliminates a smaller quantity than a large one. If a person weighs about 215 lbs. and the total solids eliminated show 1020 grains it may be considered quite normal.

Exercise influences it some, but not as much as size. Therefore the total solids vary from 700-1100 grains according to the circumstances just mentioned, and they vary inversely as the quantity of urine.

Specific Gravity in Diseases.

Increased:	Diminished:
Diabetes (saccharine),	Diabetes (insipidus),
Acute niphritis,	Chronic kidney trouble,
Febrile disturbances.	Many nervous disorders.

The reaction—The reaction of normal urine is mildly acid. The acidity is mainly due to the sodium acid phosphate which is held in solution, however it may become neutral or feebly alkaline during digestion. The reaction is taken with litmus paper. A small piece of it is moistened with the urine, and if blue paper is turned red the urine is acid in reaction, but if the red paper is turned blue it is alkaline, and if neither paper is changed in color it is neutral. Urine that is secreted shortly after a meal usually is alkaline in reaction, this is known as the alkaline tide. After meals or at intervals between meals, it may regain its acidity or even increase its degree, this is known as the acid tide. On standing a few hours, usually the urine increases in acidity due to the so-called acid fermentation. This is followed by a gradual diminution in acidity to a neutral and later to an alkaline reaction due to the ammonical fermentation. Therefore when the urine is mixed for 24 hours it is generally of mildly acid reaction.

There are two theories regarding these tides. Jones' theory is, that the acids in the stomach are converted into the carbonates which alkalinize the urine. The other, Roberts theory, is, that the alkaline food is absorbed by the blood and so directly alkalinizes the urine.

One person may pass a strongly acid and another a mildly acid urine on the same diet. Animal diet has a tendency to increase the acidity, whereas a vegetable diet tends to diminish it or render it alkaline due to the fact that the salts of potassium and sodium which are found in vegetables are converted into the carbonates and render the urine alkaline.

All mineral acids tend to increase the acidity when given in large doses. The vegetables acids, when taken into the system are oxidized into carbon dioxid and water, and therefore fail to have any marked effect, either no affect or slightly increase the degree of acidity, but never do they alkalinize it.

The benzine acids are not destroyed by oxidation and are eliminated by the kidney and acidify the urine to a marked degree.

All bodies which are alkaline in reaction, when taken internally alkalinize the urine. The chief ones are the hydroxides, carbonates, borates and another class which is neutral in reaction outside of the body though taken into the system are converted into the alkaline carbonates. These are the compounds of calcium, sodium, magnesium, lithium and potassium made with vegetable acids.   There is one exception, if potassium or sodium bicarbonate is given during meals it alkalinizes the urine, but if given between meals it increases its acidity.

The degree of acidity may be ascertained by determining the amount of an alkaline solution of known strength required to neutralize the acidity of the specimen.   One tenth normal solution of sodium hydrate is usually taken as the alkaline solution, and one degree of acidity means that one c.c. of this solution neutralizes the acid in 100 c.c. of urine.   The normal varies between 30 and 40 degrees.

Reaction in Diseases.

Increased:	Diminished:
Rheumatism,	Anaemia,
Gout,	General debility,
Saccharine diabetes,	Persistent vomiting.
Chronic nephritis,	
Febrile disturbances.	

Urea is held in solution in the normal urine, and is derived in part from the unused proteids of the food and in part from the physiological waste of the body. This is brought to the kidneys by the blood in the form of urea.

The amount excreated in health varies from 300-600 grains or 1.5 to 2.6% dependent upon the amount of exercise and the quantity and quality of food taken.

Urea is

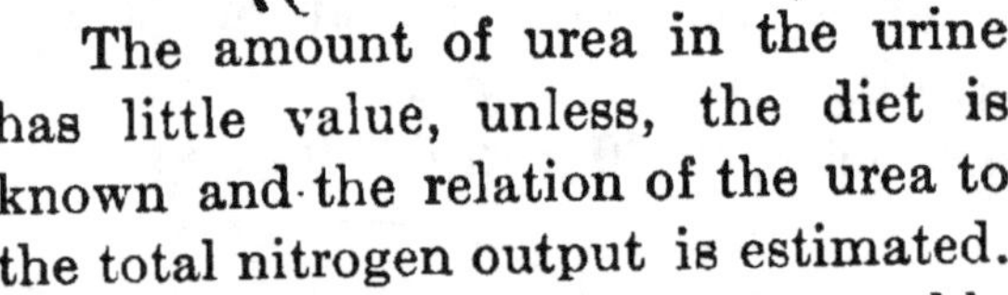

Increased:
Meat diet,
Febrile disturbances,
Diabetes and after epilep-
   tic attacks,
Phosphorous and arsenic
   poisoning.

Diminished:
Vegetable diet,
During fasting,
Gout,
Kidney disorders,
Uremia.

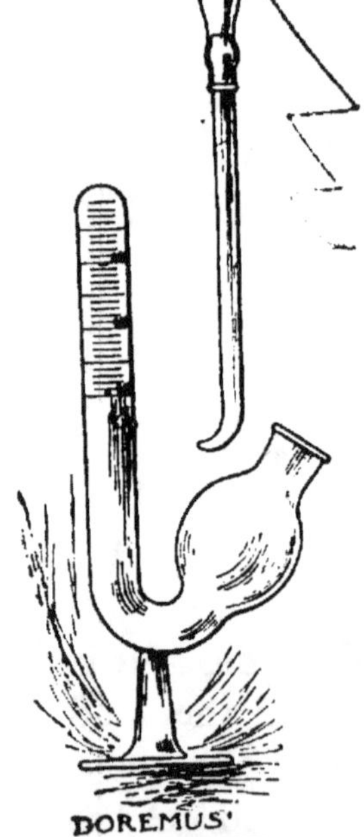

DOREMUS'
UREOMETER

The amount of urea in the urine has little value, unless, the diet is known and the relation of the urea to the total nitrogen output is estimated.

The urea test therefore only roughly indicates that the kidney is doing its proper work. Urine for this test should be fresh, as when decomposition sets in there is a gradual decrease in the amount of urea.

The quantity of urea may be estimated with the "ureometer." It consists of a specially constructed U shaped glass tube with graduations on the long arm and a dilated bulb on the shorter, and a pipette capable of measuring one cubic centimeter.

The method of using the instrument is as follows: Make a solution of 4 grams of sodium hydroxide in 10 c.c. of water. This should be shaken occasionally until it is all disolved and cold.

Then add one c.c. of bromine and shake again.

This is known as sodium hypobromite solution. Care should be taken to avoid coming in contact with the fumes of the bromine as these are very irritating. Pour enough of this solution into the ureometer to fill the long arm and the bend, so that no air remains in the tube. Then draw one c.c. of urine into the pipette by the attached bulb, passing the curved beak well into the bend of the long arm and slowly introduce the urine when an effervescent reaction occurs.

$$CO\,(N\,H_2)_2\,3\,(Na\,Br) = 3\,Na\,Br\,C\,O_2\,2H_2O\,2N.$$

The urea is being decomposed, nitrogen gas which is liberated collects at the top of the long arm of the tube, the graduations indicate the per cent, or, each division indicates 0.001 gramme of urea for one c.c. of urine. If it is less than the normal amount, it indicates that there is a retention in the system of poisonous products which should have been eliminated. If it is more than normal, then the loss is greater than the gain and the metabolism is accordingly going down.

Chlorides—The chlorides which are found in the urine are derived almost entirely from the chlorides in the food eaten, chiefly in the form of sodium chloride (common salt). Ordinarily healthy persons pass from 150 to 175 grains in 24 hours but it is subject to considerable variation.

They are increased; by drinking large amounts of water, by increased ingestion of common salt, during the first few days after the crisis of acute febrile diseases, after epileptic attacks, during the rapid absorption of large effusions.

They are diminished: During repose, in acute febrile diseases up to the time of crisis, during the for-

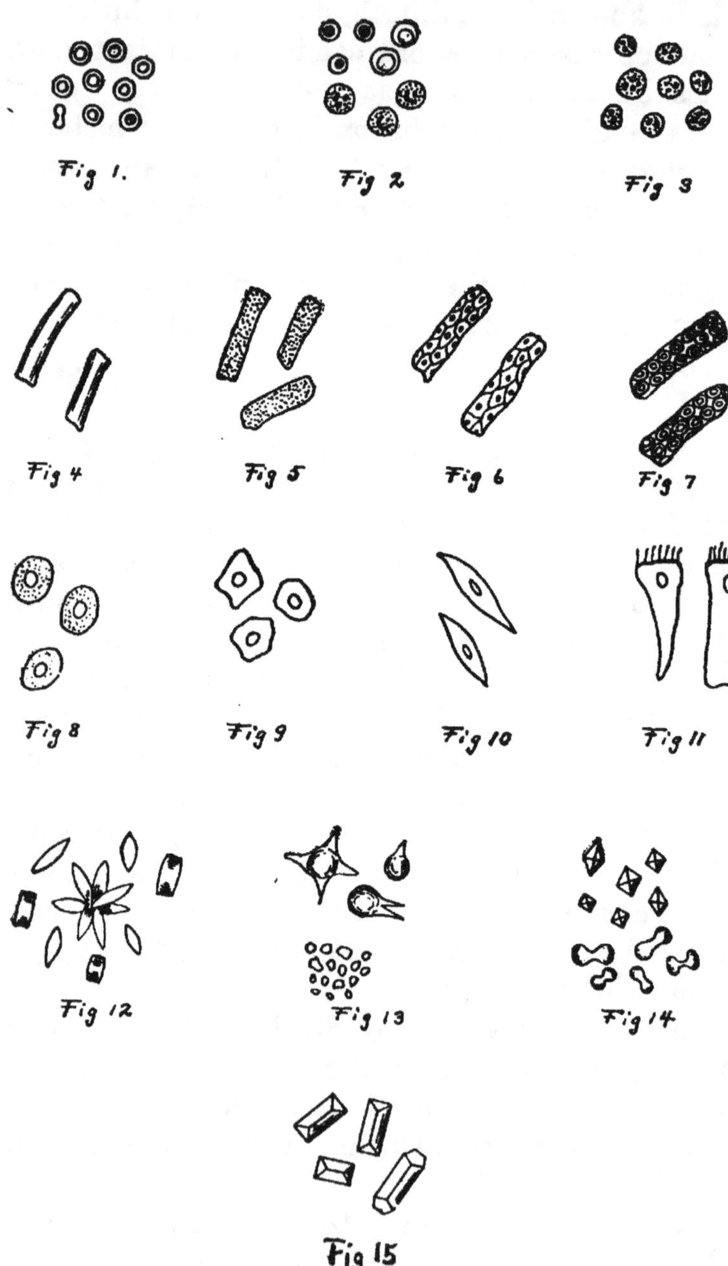

Fig 1.
Fig 2
Fig 3
Fig 4
Fig 5
Fig 6
Fig 7
Fig 8
Fig 9
Fig 10
Fig 11
Fig 12
Fig 13
Fig 14
Fig 15

mation of large exudates, diarrhoea, anaemia, kidney lesions.

Test—To a little urine in a test tube add a solution of silver nitrate, both chlorides and phosphates are precipitated; upon the addition of nitric acid the phosphatic precipitate is redissolved leaving the silver chloride unaffected, though readily dissolved in ammonia. If absent no precipitate will form.

Phosphates—The phosphates consist partly in earthy, and partly in alkaline phosphates.

The earthy phosphates are those of calcium and magnesium. They are insoluble in water but soluble in acids and so are held in solution in acid urine, but are precipitated when the urine becomes neutral or alkaline in reaction.

When urine undergoes decomposition, the carbonate of ammonia which is formed from the urea combines with the magnesium phosphate and forms the crystaline ammonio-magnesium-phosphate or triple phosphate.

The alkaline phosphates consist of sodium and potassium phosphate. They are soluble in water not precipitated from solution when the urine is rendered alkaline. The phosphates like the chlorides are mainly derived from the food and the daily elimination varies from 30 to 45 grains.

They are increased:
By ingestion of phosphates and phosphoric acid, by excessive nitrogenous diet, by any nervous strain, in inflammatory diseases, rheumatism, and extensive bone disease.

They are decreased:
During pregnancy, Melancholia, exhaustion, kidney lesions, dyspepsia and pneumonia.

Test. (See test for chlorides.)

A very convenient way is to take two test tubes of equal diameter and pour into them equal quantities of urine. Add a few drops of silver nitrate solution to each; both phosphates and chlorides will be precipitated. Then add nitric acid to one and set the tubes aside a few minutes to allow the precipitate to fall to the bottom. The one will contain the chlorides and the phosphates and will be the greater bulk, and the other the chlorides only; since the nitric acid dissolved the phosphates. If the precipitate is equal in bulk then the phosphates are absent.

Indican is present in the urine only in minute quantities, but if it is present in large quantities, it is of clinical significance. If it is present in large amounts it may give to the urine a bluish color.

Indican is derived from indol, a product which is formed in the intestines by the putrefaction of proteid food. When this indol comes in contact with the acids of the urine it is broken up and unites with the potassium sulphate and indigo is formed.

Indigo is found in the urine when there is a rapid decomposition of intestinal contents, as in peritonitis, obstruction of the small intestines and in diseases of the liver which interfere with the formation of bile.

It has also been found in suppurative and gangrenous condition of other parts of the body as for example in empyema, gangrene or abscess of the lung, and in appendiceal abscess.

It has also been observed after the administration of turpentine or creosote. It is therefore an indicator that there is absorption of putrefactive substances, showing a certain toxaemia.

Jaffe's Test—Take equal volumes of urine and fuming hydrochloric acid, and then, with constant shaking, add drop by drop a saturated solution of chloride of lime until the greatest intensity of blue color is reached. It is then shaken with chloroform, which will dissolve the indican and separate from the solution, colored blue.

The amount of coloring will indicate the amount of indican present.

Average Composition of Urine.

Organic

Water	949.25
Urea	26.00
Creatine	Traces
Creatinine	1.50
Sodium and Potassium urates	1.75
Free uric acid	Traces
Mucus and coloring matter	.25

Inorganic

Sodium acid phosphate	
Calcium and Magnesium	6.25
Sodium and Potassium chlorides	9.25
Sodium and Potassium sulphates	5.75
	1000.00

ABNORMAL URINE.

Urine may be abnormal in three ways.

1. Through its containing substances that are entirely foreign to it, e. g. albumin or sugar.

2. To an altered proportion of its constituents, as too much or not enough of urea or chlorides.

3. Normal constituents in an abnormal form, as when uric acid is found as a solid which should be in solution.

The analysis of urine may be divided into two parts:

1. The detection of substances held in solution.

2. The examination of any deposit that may be present.

The Detection of Abnormal Substances Held in Solution.

The most important abnormal substances held in solution are albumin, sugar and bile. The presence of albumin in the urine is known as albuminuria, although it may not necessarily mean serious organic disturbance of the kidneys, still it always points to some urinary or systemic disorder, and its presence, however slight demands consideration.

Albuminuria is divided into two classes (1) True or Renal. (2) False, or Infra Renal. True albuminuria is that which is due to the escape of a portion of the albuminous part of the blood into the tubules with the water and salts of the urine.

False albuminuria is that when albumin is mixed

with the urine during its passage through the urinary tract, which is derived from the blood, pus, or secretions that contain albumin.

Urine that contains albumin is considered pathologic. Albuminous urine is usually pale and of low specific gravity and the amount eliminated varies considerably.

True albuminuria may be:

1. Non Nephritic.
    (1) Non Pathologic.
     (a) Physiologic.
     (b) Cyclic.
     (c) New born.
     (d) Pregnancy or Parturition.

    (2) Pathologic.
     (a) Febrile disturbances.
     (b) Blood changes.
     (c) Diseased nervous system.
     (d) Diseases of the alimentary tract.
     (e) Inflamation of the urinary tract.

2. Nephritic.
     (a) Acute Nephritis.
     (b) Chronic Nephritis, or Bright's disease.

Physiologic albuminuria is the presence of albumin in the urine, where no gross lesion of the kidney can be found but the malpighian bodies are too weak to hold back the albuminous part of the blood and allow it to pass through. This is known as glomerular insufficiency. It may also be caused by severe muscular exertion, bath, meal, cold, or nervous excitement.

Cyclic albuminuria is that in which small quantities of albumin appear at certain times of the day, or at certain periods. In the new-born it may be cyclic, and usually due to the ingestion of certain forms of food. May also be seen during adolescence.

In pregnancy, it may be due to overdistention of the uterus which produces pressure upon the kidneys and interferes with the circulation. It may also be caused by the changes in the blood due to maternal and fetal metabolism, and usually disappears after labor. This may be due to severe muscular exertion of labor. These are physiological, the following pathological:

In fevers, the presence of albumin is caused by slight changes in the glomeruli due to the high temperature of the body and the disturbances of nutrition induced by the toxic material which is produced by the different bacteria in the system. In these cases parenchymatous degeneration is always found.

Blood changes, as purpura, scurvy, anaemia, leukemia, lead or mercury poisoning, or the presence of bile or sugar in the blood may cause the passage of small amounts of albumin.

In nervous disorders, as after an attack of epilepsy, apoplexy, or mental fatigue, albumin may be present for a short time. In disorders of the alimentary tract, putrefactive changes in the intestines create toxins which irritate the kidneys and allow albumin to pass.

Before applying any test, care should be taken that the urine is perfectly clear, and if it is turbid from any cause, it should be filtered.

Nitric acid test.—The most reliable tests for albumin are the nitric acid and the heat tests. Allow 20 or 30 drops of nitric acid to gently trickle down the side of a test tube containing about two drams of urine, while holding the tube inclined at an angle of about 45 degrees. The acid being the heavier will flow to the bottom. If albumin is present an opaque white layer will appear where the urine and acid meet, and this does not clear up on the application of heat. Mucus, especially when the urine is concentrated and cold, forms a white cloud resembling albumin, but it is higher up where the acid is weak, since the strong acid solution dissolves it. The urates may be thrown out of solution, but these will disappear on gentle heating.

Heat test—Fill a test tube 2-3 full of urine, and if alkaline or neutral in reaction, render it feebly acid by adding a drop or two of acetic acid, but if already acid none need be added. Then heat only the upper part to boiling so that it may readily be compared with the lower part if any reaction should occur. If albumin is present, a diffuse white cloud will appear. If a turbidity occurs, it may be due to the earthy phosphates, but these will disappear upon the addition of nitric acid while albumin will not. If no white cloud forms on heating, no albumin is present. In order to be positive as to the presence or absence of albumin, it is best in all cases to confirm the results of the one test by the other.

Quantitative test—Use Esbach's graduated test tube and fill to mark U with filtered urine, then to mark R with the reagent, then mix thoroughly and let stand for 24 hours. The albumin will be deposited at the bottom of the tube and the quantity is read off in tenths of one percent.

The reagent for this test is

 10 gm Picric ac.
 20 gm Citric ac.
1000 c.c Aqua dest.

Sugar—Sugar is constantly found in the urine of patients who are affected with diabetes mellitus. Such urine is light in color almost like water. It has a sweetish odor and rapidly ferments when it is kept in a warm place. The reaction is acid, and the specific gravity high, ranging from 1025-1040. The quantity of urine passed may vary from 4-20 pints. It has been observed for only a short time after chloroform narcosis, cholera and injuries of the brain, excessive mental exertion and excessive emotional activity, as grief, worry and shock.

Test.—The most reliable tests for sugar in the urine are Haines' test, and the fermentation test.

Haines' Sugar Test Solution.

Copper Sulphate .... gr. 30
Pure water .... fl. oz. ½
Make perfect solution and add
 Glycerine .... fl. oz. ½
Mix well and add
 Liquor potassae .... fl. oz. 5

This should give a perfectly clear, transparent, dark blue liquid, which may be kept any length of time. It may throw down a slight reddish deposit after standing several weeks, but this does not affect its value as a test.

The test is performed as follows:

Take about one dram of this solution and gently boil it, when no reaction should take place, now add six or eight drops of urine and boil again a few seconds. If sugar is present an abundant yellow or reddish yellow precipitate is thrown down. If sugar is absent no change will take place.

Roberts' fermentation test.—Urine that ferments contains sugar, and the urine will lose in specific gravity after fermentation is completed.

Take two bottles filled with urine and set side by side to assume the same temperature. One bottle is corked tightly, and the other loosely, or not at all and little yeast is added. Then both are set aside and kept at a warm temperature. After 24 hours fermentation will be completed, then take the specific gravity of each. Each degree of difference in the specific gravity will correspond to one grain of sugar for every fluid ounce.

For instance, if the specific gravity of the unfermented urine, or before fermentation was 1030 and after fermentation it is 1010, it will have contained 20 grains of sugar to the fluid ounce. To determine whether or not fermentation has ceased, test the urine for sugar, as long as it gives the reaction for sugar fermentation is not completed.

Bile—Biliary coloring matter occurs in the urine in different forms of jaundice. The color of the urine which contains bile varies from a yellowish-brown or greenish-yellow to nearly pure green. The urine foams easily on shaking and the foam possesses a yellow tint. If a piece of filter paper or linen be moistened with such urine, it retains a permanent yellow color on drying.

Test.—Take several drams of urine in a test tube and allow 20 to 30 drops of nitric acid to gently trickle down the side of the tube. In the presence of bile a greenish color will develop where the urine and acid meet.

Gmelin's test.—Place several drops of urine on a porcelain dish and several drops of fuming nitric acid alongside of it. When the two are brought in contact a play of colors is observed, commencing with green and blue changing to violet and red, and finally to a brownish color.

Acetone is a colorless liquid with a peculiar ethereal, fruity odor. It may be present in minute quantities in health, and the significance of acetone in the urine is not very great unless it is present in large quantities. It is formed in the body by the decomposition of albuminoid material, and occurs in the urine in fevers, starvation, auto-intoxication, diabetes, especially in diabetic coma, and if found during pregnancy, it is suggestive of a dead fetus.

Test.—A convenient test for acetone, which is very sensitive and will not give misleading results in the presence of creatinin, alcohol or aldehyde, is the following: One-half to one c.c. of glacial acetic acid is added to fifteen c.c. of the suspected urine and a few drops of fresh nitroprusside of soda solution are added. Then a few c.c. of ammonia are carefully floated on the surface and if acetone is present an intense violet ring will appear at the line of contact of the fluids.

The Origin and Effects of the Fixed and Volatile Alkaline Urine.

When urine is left standing at a warm temperature it gives off a strong odor, becomes turbid and decidedly alkaline in reaction. The microbes in the urine (micrococcus ureae) produce a substance called emsein and the emsein acts upon the urea and converts it into carbonate of ammonia which is alkaline in reaction. This renders the urine alkaline and turbid, and gives it a peculiar putrid ammoniacal odor. This reaction is called the ammoniacal fermentation. That which occurs in the urine out of the body may also occur in the bladder, and cause great disturbance. This may be induced by the introduction of bacteria into the bladder with unclean instruments, especially the catheter.

A healthy bladder will sweep out all microbes during micturition, but if the bladder lining is injured or inflamed the microbes will be retained and set up this ammoniacal fermentation. There are therefore two causes of ammoniacal urine. Infection of the bladder, and the retention of microbes.

The fixed alkalies, as referred to the urine, are the carbonates of potassium and sodium. The volatile alkalies, are the compounds of ammonium. When the urine is alkaline in reaction, to determine whether or not its alkalinity depends upon the fixed or the volatile alkalies proceed as follows: Take a little urine in a test tube and slightly warm it to about 80° or 85° F. but no more, then take a piece of red litmus paper and moisten it in water and hold it above the test tube.

If the alkalinity is due to the volatile alkalies the red litmus paper will be turned blue and will assume its original red color on drying. If it is due to the fixed alkalies the red litmus will not be changed. However, if it is moistened with the urine the color is permanently changed blue.

Ammoniacal urine is secreted acid, but is converted in the bladder by ammoniacal fermentation into volatile alkaline urine. Fixed alkaline urine is secreted alkaline. Ammoniacal urine points to local trouble, the fixed, points to general disturbance or to medication. Ammoniacal urine is highly irritating, fixed alkaline urine is mild and non-irritating. Ammoniacal urine precipitates the earthy phosphates in a crystalline form (triple phosphates), the fixed alkali precipitates them in an amorphous form. Ammoniacal urine has a tendency to form calculi, fixed alkaline urine does not have this tendency.

Urine that is turbid from chemical substances will clear itself on standing, but if the turbidity is due to microbic action it will not clear itself, but it increases. Alkaline urine precipitates earthy phosphates under all conditions, and the sediment is white, while acid urine precipitates the urates, the sediment having a light pink color especially if the urine is concentrated and cold.

Effects of Nitric Acid on the Urine.

1. Gases evolved: Nitrogen, Carbon Dioxide (if urine contains carbonates).

2. Deposits: Albumin, Mucin, Urates, Urea.

3. Colors produced: Red (normal), Greenish (bile), Dark Blue (indican).

Effects of Potassium Hydroxid.

1. When cold, it precipitates the earthy phosphates.

2. When hot, in the presence of sugar, it gives a dark brown color.

3. Clears up the urates.

4. Clears up uric acid.

5. Prevents coagulation of albumin by heat.

6. Gelatinizes in the presence of pus.

7. Dark brown precipitate of phosphates in the presence of blood or biliary coloring matter.

Effects of Acetic Acid.

1. Precipitates mucus.

2. Precipitates urates.

3. Clears up the earthy phosphates.

Turbidity of Urine.

Due to phosphates:

1. Sediment white;
2. Reaction alkaline;
3. Clears up on the addition of an acid;
4. Frequently precipitated when heated.

Due to urates:

1. Sediment pink;
2. Reaction acid;
3. Clears up on the addition of an alkali;
4. Clears up by g e n t l e heat.

EXAMINATION OF DEPOSITS.

The urine should be allowed to settle in a conical glass for several hours or a specimen should be centrifuged and the sediment removed with a pipette, placed on a clean slide and covered with a clean cover glass, for microscopic examination.

Casts—A urinary cast is a mass of fibrinous or plastic material that has taken the form of the tubule in which it has been moulded. They are produced by the admission into the tubules of a coagulable constituent of the blood, or from the tubules, by the disintegration and fusion of the epithelial lining. When this becomes detached it slips out of the tubules into the ureter and bladder and is voided in the urine. They are perhaps the most important findings of a microscopic examination, because they always indicate a degenerative process of the kidneys, and are nearly always associated with the presence of albumin.

There are three classes of casts, the cellular, granular and the structureless. The first consists chiefly of cellular elements, as epithelial cells, red blood corpuscles and leucocytes. Epithelial casts (Fig. 6), like all other casts, are tube-like cylinders, consisting of epithelial cells. When it consists chiefly of red or white blood corpuscles it is called a ''blood cast'' (Fig. 7), and found in renal haemorrhage and in acute haemorrhagic nephritis.

The granular casts consist of fine or coarse granules which result from degenerative changes of the epithelial cells lining the tubules. These may also be formed by like changes of the red or white blood corpuscles. Casts which contain oil drops, are called "oil-casts," or "fatty casts" (Fig. 5), which are indicative of fatty degeneration of the kidney.

The structureless casts, which are of doubtful value, consist of a homogeneous material, clear as water with a very faint outline often difficult to see. A variety of hyaline casts which have a yellowish appearance resembling wax, are called "waxy casts." (Fig. 4.)

Casts vary in length and breadth. The ends appear broken off, rounded or irregular. The color varies somewhat, depending upon the amount of the granular or other material which they contain.

Pus—Pus in the urine may come from any part of the urinary tract and its presence is a very important symptom. Urine which contains pus is usually turbid when voided and rapidly deposits a yellowish white sediment on standing. This after some time becomes stringy and viscid. Such urine may be acid in reaction, when voided, but it may be alkaline in affections of the bladder or soon becomes so after being voided. The sediment may be mistaken for phosphates or urates, but the phosphates will rapidly disappear on the addition of an acid and the urates on the application of gentle heat while purulent urine deposits albumin.

In testing for pus allow the sediment to subside, decant the upper part and pour the deposit into a test tube, then add half its bulk of liquor potassae and shake; if pus is present, the mixture will become thick and gelatinous which is more manifest as the mixture is poured from one test tube to another.

Pus is the liquified product of suppurative inflammation, and consists of cells and an albuminous fluid. A pus cell is a broken down leucocyte and appears under the microscope as a small, granular, spherical cell somewhat larger than a corpuscle. When acetic acid is added the fragments become more distinct. (Fig. 3.)

Blood—Urine that contains blood is of a light red to a deep red color, and usually of alkaline reaction. Blood on long contact with the urine becomes dark on account of oxidation.

The blood may be derived from a diseased condition of any part of the urinary tract, as in acute nephritis, cystitis or severe cases of gonorrhoea, from toxic material circulating in the blood, or from the introduction of instruments into the urethra. Urine that contains blood may give the reaction of albumin, but this albumin is that which is found in the blood.

Test.—Take equal parts of freshly prepared tincture of guaiac and ozonized (old) spirits of turpentine and mix it well, and cautiously float it over some urine in a test tube. In the presence of blood it will give a blue line where the urine and the mixture come in contact.

When examined under the microscope red and white corpuscles will be found. The red corpuscles are circular, bi-concave discs, having a light yellowish color. The corpuscles usually adhere to each other and form rolls or columns, resembling coin. (Fig. 1.) The white corpuscles or leucocytes are rounded or spherical nucleated bodies, having a slightly granular appearance. (Fig. 2.) The leucocytes may easily be mistaken for pus corpuscles, but a pus corpuscle is larger, and more granular than a leucocyte and the outline is somewhat irregular and the nucleus fragmented.

Epithelial cells—Epithelial cells from the urinary

tract are found in the urine under normal circumstances, in small amounts but when they are present in large quantities they signify a circulatory or inflammatory disturbance.

There are four chief varieties: 1, Round cells (Fig. 8.) 2. Spindle cells. (Fig. 10.) 3. Squamous cells. (Fig. 9.) 4. Columnar cells. (Fig. 11.)

The round cells arise from the tubules and the deeper layer of the mucus membrane of the bladder, urethra and pelvis of the kidney. They are a little larger than the leucocytes. Spindle cells, are derived from the superficial layers of the pelvis of the kidney, ureters and the urethra. Squamous cells are usually derived from the bladder or the vagina. If they are present in large amounts, it usually indicates a cystitis. Columnar cells are derived from the superficial layers of the pelvis of the kidney, ureters and urethra. All of these cells may vary somewhat in their form. They have a granular appearance and a distinct nucleus.

Calcium Oxalate—Calcium oxalate crystals are found in acid urine. They are held in solution by the acids of the urine, but when these become deficient, they are precipitated and caught in the mucus of the urine which may form a slight cloud.

The quantity varies from .01 to .02 gramme in 24 hours. The amount eliminated depends upon the diet, and it is increased when such fruits which contain oxalic acid as rhubarb, tomatoes, cabbage or apples are taken therefore the diet is an important factor. They are also found when there is an incomplete oxidation of sugars or fats, in disorders of the stomach and intestines, dyspepsia, neurasthenia and frequently in connection with neuralgic pains, wasting diseases as tuberculosis and cancer.

They appear under the microscope in the form of octahedra and dumb bell crystals. The octahedra crystals resemble a four sided pyramid, or a square crossed by two bright diagonal lines. The dumb bell crystals are so named on account of their form, and are less frequently met with than the octahedra. (Fig. 14.)

These crystals are insoluble in water, alkalies and acetic acid, but soluble in hydrochloric acid. Uric acid crystals dissolve when an alkali is added and the triple phosphates dissolve on the addition of acetic acid.

Phosphates—The phosphates have already been referred to, so we will consider here only the microscopic appearance. The triple phosphates or ammonio-magnesium phosphates form a crystalline deposit in the form of a triangular prism with bevelled ends. They are perfectly clear and colorless. (Fig. 15.) Calcium phosphate occurs in the form of amorphous grains or in conical wedge shaped crystals, so that when they are properly arranged will form a rosette. (Fig. 13.)

Uric acid—Crystals of uric acid are found perfect in acid urine only. They present or assume a great variety of forms, but as a rule they are lozenge shaped, in the form of four sided prisms or knife blades. (Fig. 12.) They have a reddish or yellowish red color and dissolve on the addition of alkalies.

Uric acid is almost insoluble in water and does not occur in normal urine as uric acid, but in the form of soluble urates chiefly as sodium and ammonium urates. However, uric acid may be liberated from its compounds and be precipitated in its characteristic crystalline form during the period of acid fermentation. In normal urine the urates are held in solution, however, when there is an increased acidity, the urine, though clear on being voided, on becoming cold will precipitate sodium urate in the form of a heavy deposit of pink or reddish brown granules, known as gravel or brick dust deposit. A precipitate of urates will clear up on heating while other sediments will not.

Sodium urate appears under the microscope as pale pink or dark red granules. They may be distributed throughout the field of observation or they may become adherent to each other by shreds of mucus and form short strings which may easily be mistaken for granular casts. However, the application of heat or acetic acid will dissolve the urates whereas a granular cast will not change. Ammonium urates are precipitated as reddish or brownish balls from which fine needles project resembling a thorn apple. These are always found in alkaline urine during the period of alkaline fermentation. (Fig. 13.)

Bacteria—A great variety of bacteria may be found in the urine, such are the bacteria of certain infectious diseases as typhoid fever, pneumonia, gonorrhea or tuberculosis. They escape from the blood and are eliminated with the urine. Besides these are found the bacteria of decomposition as the micrococcus ureae. The most important bacteria are the streptococci and the diplococci especially where catherization has been practiced. They appear under the microscope as very small round bodies or rods in clumps or chains.

Ehrlich's Diazo-reaction—The diazo-reaction was introduced by Ehrlich in 1882 as a urinary test of great value in typhoid fever. During the course of the disease certain substances are formed and eliminated with the urine, which when brought into contact with Ehr-lich's reagent produce a certain characteristic reaction.

This is performed as follows: take 3 c.c. of urine in a test tube, add one drop of a $\frac{1}{2}\%$ solution of sodium nitrite and shake. Then add 3 c.c. of a saturated solution of sulphanilic acid in 5% hydrochloric acid and shake. Then allow 3 c.c. of ammonium hydroxide to trickle down the side of the test tube and this will produce a red ring where the ammonia and mixture meet. On shaking the test tube the urine will turn to a port wine color and the foam will be pink. If the test is negative the change of colors will not appear. It is at times, but rarely found in measles, pyæmia, scarlet fever, and miliary tuberculosis. In these the foam is not pink but yellow or orange.

CATHETERIZATION.

It frequently happens that patients experience considerable difficulty in passing the urine after an operation or confinement, while in the recumbent position and may have to be relieved by catheterization. However, this is frequently not necessary and may be avoided by making hot applications over the bladder or to the vulva. Sometimes the sound of water trickling into the bed pan will bring on urination spontaneously. If the patient can pass it voluntarily she should be permitted to do so, but if the applications have failed to produce the desired effect and no urine has been passed from 8-12 hours she should be catheterized as follows: Remove the bed clothes and expose the vulva under good light, so as to bring the urethral opening into full view by separating the labia with the thumb and forefinger of the left hand. With the right hand rinse off the vulva and urethral meatus with sterile water or clean it with a cotton swab and boric acid or $\frac{1}{2}\%$ lysol solution. Then take the catheter from the vessel without touching its vesical end and gently introduce it into the bladder allowing it to follow its own direction. Before withdrawing the catheter, stop up its outer end with the forefinger to prevent the urine from dribbling over the parts and air entering the bladder, then gently withdraw.

Glass catheters are the best for women because they are more easily kept clean and aseptic. Before and after use, the catheter should be well cleansed and boiled for not less than five minutes, and when not in use should be kept in a 5% carbolic acid solution with some cotton at the bottom of the vessel to prevent breaking the catheter.

Before introducing it, see if it has any cracks, and if it has it must be discarded, because if any pieces drop out and fall into the bladdder it may give rise to serious consequences. The introduction of mucus from the vulva or vagina into the bladder may cause a cystitis. If after the introduction of an unclean catheter into the bladder, a cystitis has resulted, the patient will begin to complain of frequent urination and a burning pain along the urethra. Pain over the pubic or iliac regions, or it may be referred to the neck of the bladder or perinaeum. Spasms of the bladder may develop. The urine becomes turbid, fetid and alkaline in reaction due to ammoniacal fermentation.

Treatment—Rest in bed, a bland non-irritating diet,

such as milk and alkaline mineral waters freely. Urinary antiseptics, such as urotropin and salol, hot applications over the bladder, and daily irrigations with 2% boric acid solution, 1-2000 potassium permanganate solution, or sometimes a dram of oil of cloves to a half gallon of a saturated boric acid solution.